The Writers' Block is a space dedicated to creative writing and story. Newly based in The Ladder in Redruth, it is a space of welcome where words and language enrich and empower, particularly those at the margins of society. By increasing enjoyment, skills and confidence in the written and spoken word, we strengthen our Cornish community and build the future we need. We nourish emerging and established writers and performers whose impact will be felt across Cornwall and beyond.
thewritersblock.org.uk

Designed & printed in Cornwall.
First print 2023.
All rights reserved.

This book or any portion thereof may not be reproduced or used in any manner whatsoever without the express written permission of the copyright holder except for the use of brief quotations in a book review. This includes the photographs and illustrations.

Photo credits

The Writers' Block	Steve Tanner
Stories of Stuff	Ruby Ingleheart
Agents 4 Change	Thomas Norris
Stret an Levow	Josh Morse

Illustrations

Cover Illustration	Redruth Press
Stret an Levow map	Sue Hill
The Writers' Block door	Keith Sparrow

Book Design

Erwin van Wanrooij	DutchDesign.Company

Contents

INTRODUCTION 4
Amanda Harris

A LIBRARY OF LOST STORIES 6
Joshua Nawras and Felix Mortimer

STORIES OF STUFF 8
You Don't Mess With My Mother 9
Sarah Connors
Underneath I'm Smiling 10
Annamaria Murphy
Labrys: The Double Axe 11
Annamaria Murphy

PROJECT RE 12
Sarah Perry and Sara Clasper

OPEN LETTER TO REDRUTH 16
Agents 4 Change
Redruth 19
Mo
I hate you... 19
Alice

MESKLA | BREWYON DRUDH 20
Sovay Berriman

REDRUTH PRESS 26
Tony Minnion and Caroline Wilkins

15 DRAUGHTS LATER 30
Ollie Mcfarlane and James Darcy
Operation Goodnight 31
Ollie Mcfarlane

TREASURES OF REDRUTH 32
Phil Kincaid

STRET AN LEVOW STREET OF VOICES 37
Prodigal Son 38
Sue Hill
Emily Knuckey and the Carpet 40
Annamaria Murphy

CONTRIBUTOR BIOGRAPHIES 42

THANKS AND FUNDERS 47

Redruth Story Book

One of my favourite words is 'serendipity' - the fact of something interesting or pleasant happening by chance — or even better is the adjective 'serendipitous'. There are, in fact, two serendipitous encounters that have led to the creation of this book.

The first was the fact that we had to move The Writers' Block from its home in Pool back in September 2021 and needed to find a new home. We knew we wanted to be in a town and had our fingers crossed for Redruth.

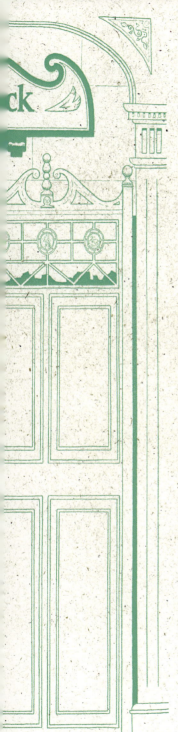

THE WRITERS' BL☐CK

Then we encountered Josh and Felix from RIFT who were hoping to take on the lease of the former library in Redruth – could we too have a space in that beautiful and august building? In short, the answer was yes and we opened our doors in late January 2023 in the building now called The Ladder. A key attraction being that this is a much-loved community resource and we wanted to build on that. We developed a community project called Stories of Stuff so that people could start to get to know us, with the aim that we could exhibit the collected stories in The Ladder for people to enjoy when they visit. We have also added some of the stories into The Story Republic repertoire to share in performance. This was all so well received that we began to think about what next.

This led to the next serendipitous encounter with Sarah Clasper from Make A Mends who told me in no uncertain terms that there were a lot of 'story projects' in Redruth. Which made me think that a good job for The Writers' Block would be to celebrate and showcase these projects, their wonderful stories, the creativity of the writers, artists and makers as well as the wider community and town itself.

The result is the Redruth Story Book which gives a flavour of the weird, the wonderful, the ordinary and imaginary, the reality of being young in town and a closer look at some of the beautiful buildings in and around Fore Street. We hope you enjoy it and that it adds to the sense of pride in this special place.

Amanda Harris, Editor
The Writers' Block
February 2023

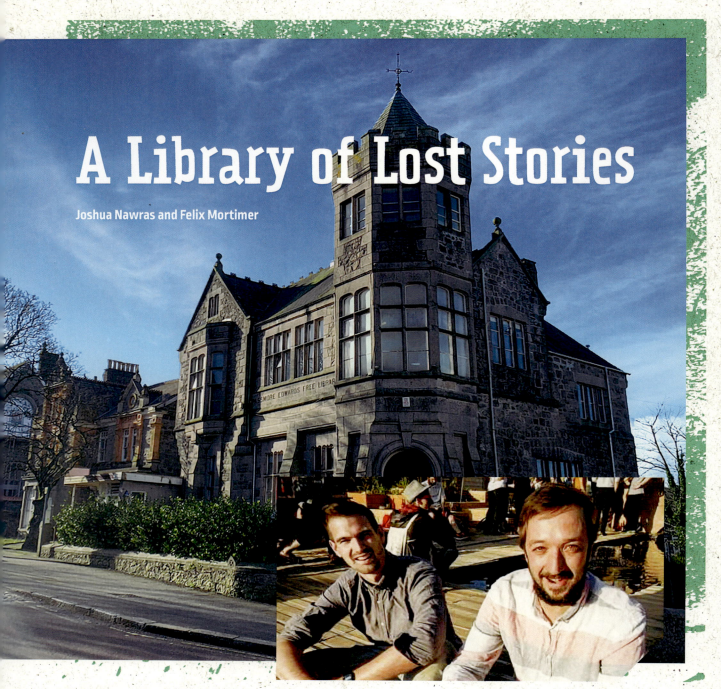

A Library of Lost Stories

Joshua Nawras and Felix Mortimer

On 18th February 2021 we fell in love with a library that had lost its stories.

On that bright February morning, the former Passmore Edwards Library in Redruth looked magnificent. All late Victorian grandeur and romantic crenellated turrets, sitting solidly on the corner of Clinton Road, looking out over Redruth as it had for the past 125 years. It had been empty since the Cornish Archive moved over to the world class Kresen Kernow and the remaining public library was folded into the Council buildings just down the road.

Walking around the building that day it was easy to imagine it full of life, children's painting still decorated peeling walls and although the shelves were now empty it felt like it was just waiting for its next occupants to throw open the doors and welcome back its people. It was a building that was so obviously full of heart, that had been a constant in the lives of every resident of Redruth for their entire lives and now it was empty, slowly beginning to crumble, slowly beginning to feel empty and purposeless. We couldn't let it fall into disrepair or commercial redevelopment or demolition, something had to be done.

For the past decade our company, RIFT, has built a reputation for building communities around spaces and breathing new life into forgotten buildings. Often we have done this by retelling classic tales, from Shakespeare to Kafka, for new audiences in interesting ways. However, over that time our practice and our interests have broadened. We have curated festivals, commissioned writers, produced dozens of other people's plays, set up music venues and community gardens - always seeking to give ownership of the experiences we nurtured to the audiences that chose to visit us. But since 2019, just before the pandemic, our last venue had fallen to the bulldozers of development - we had become homeless. Itinerant storytellers and community builders seeking a new space to fill with a new community, with new stories, with laughter and connection.

And here it was, waiting for us, a library that had lost its stories.

We don't know what tales The Ladder, as we've renamed it, will hold over the years to come. We haven't met all the people that will make it their own - but almost two years later, the doors are finally open again and the community of storytellers and intrepid explorers is beginning to build, it feels like the beginning of something, it feels like something special, but also it feels like just the next chapter. We hope to meet you soon.

Stories of Stuff was originally conceived to coincide with the opening of the renewed Writers' Block in The Ladder, the former Redruth Library. This being delayed, we had to get out and about and meet people on the street, in their houses, care homes and businesses. Part Antiques Roadshow, part story swap the aim was to shine a light on the wealth and variety of stories, memories and experiences tightly bound up in those precious objects we store in our pockets and the backs of cupboards. Precious to us but often of little monetary worth.

Stories of Stuff

Launched on St Piran's Day, our team of writers and story detectives interviewed, listened, marvelled and then squirreled the stories away for writing up. Each participant and their object was photographed.

We held two sharing events: one at Miners' Court and the other during the heatwave at Kresen Kernow, to hear the stories read with delight and panache by The Story Republic provoking memories, amazement, joy and much shared laughter.

The stories, the objects and photographs were cleverly curated into a Cabinet of Stuff which stayed in Kresen Kernow for several weeks. It will have a permanent home in The Ladder. We hope to have the opportunity to keep refreshing and renewing it.

You Don't Mess With My Mother

Sarah Connors
as told by Tim

GOD Save THE QUEEN

When I was about 16, me and my friends used to go to Trumpet's nightclub, Redruth, on a Sunday night. It was a charity disco and only 50p to get in. Mother would insist on picking us up. '10pm sharp' she would say. Inevitably I was never outside on time and she would barge into the disco, with slippers on and hair in hot curlers and drag me out by the ear.

During one such disco, the DJ played a track by the Sex Pistols. The following day, I rushed to John Oliver's record shop in Redruth to buy it. When I got home, mother took one look at the profanities on the cover, grabbed me by the ear and marched me down to the shop. She read the riot act at the poor shop assistant. 'Disgusting it is, you selling this to a young boy'. John Oliver's were infamous for their 'No Refund' policy but they immediately gave us our money back.

You don't mess with my mother.

Post note:
Tim has recently purchased the Sex Pistols album but he still hasn't told his mother.

Lead Writer: Annamaria Murphy
Writers: Sarah Connors
Keith Sparrow
Felicity Tattersall
Mark Crees
Photographer: Ruby Ingleheart
Cabinet Design: Tony Crosby
Project Manager: Tori Cannell
The Writers' Block: Amanda Harris
Helen Reynolds
Grace Davies

Underneath I'm Smiling

Annamaria Murphy

Inspired by meeting Dylan with his favourite object, a halloween mask. Written from the point of view of The Mask.

You'll have seen many like me before. I appear in every horror film, in every fright fest, on every Halloween night.
Dylan, who loves me, carries me everywhere, and in the old days, even to school. I terrified the teachers, especially the dinner ladies. At night I hang on his bedroom wall, but he can take me down and twist my grin to gurn, scream, howling laugh in the dead of night. Sometimes, I am a shield between Dylan and the world.

But I'm not really so terrible, not really so frightening, as underneath I'm smiling, like Dylan himself.

Labrys: The Double Axe

Annamaria Murphy

Men have most of the symbols of history. Flaming swords, holding worlds on their shoulders, crowns, kingdoms. They stand on most plinths, heralded for wars, greatness in business, un-greatness in business, messy business or just business.

Christmas is coming and Jo's father has been glued to the internet for near on two weeks. He's not one for shopping, let alone internet shopping, and the family are worried. But his daughter, Jo, is coming for Christmas with her partner, and this present must be right, he thinks. In his youth, such a partnership would have been frowned on, and he wells with pride when he thinks of her and all she does in the world.

On Christmas morning the family gather. The presents are under the tree. Intriguing boxes piled high.

"And this is for you darling," he says to his daughter.

It is the smallest package. Matchbox size, too small for ribbon or string.
And inside, a tiny badge, a double edged black bladed axe. The Labrys, symbol of Minoan goddesses, adopted in the 1970s by LGBTQ women as a symbol of strength and self-sufficiency.

For goddesses everywhere, whoever and wherever they might be.

Project Re

Sarah Perry and Sara Clasper

Our journey to Redruth...
During the Covid pandemic we set ourselves a daily challenge – to make something each day from materials we had lying around our houses. This led us to selling our work on a market stall in Falmouth with a difference – as craftivists (combination of crafting and activism) we wanted to raise awareness about environmental issues – nothing new is needed. Conversations around mending began here. The community started to donate clothes to us, and we became particularly interested in repairing clothes in a creative way, often referred to as visible mending.

We started to dream about having our own premises where we could share our love of mending, recycling, crafting and community action. A friend, Liz Moody, had a workshop in the Buttermarket and we set up a stall outside on Saturday's market day. We became very fond of the community and the architecture of the town and started to look at shops for rent on Fore Street. Redruth became an obvious choice, knowing about Redruth's rich history in

textiles and its current regeneration. One day in January 2022, we happened upon the Wooden Box coffee shop and the proprietor mentioned the shop next door was available to let. We peered in the window, and were thrilled to find out it was already an established sewing and repair shop. Our friend, Liz, said she'd also like to be part of the shop and came up with the best name for our enterprise...

So, we opened Make A Mends in May with a beautiful traditional shop sign, created by a local signwriter, Jade Francesca Blacker, and a grant from Redruth Unlimited. Our manifesto captures the values central to our business.

We received a grant from Redruth Unlimited, FEAST and Cornwall Community Foundation, to research the history of repairing and recycling in Redruth town centre and to engage with current traders on these issues. We're asking them to think of a word beginning with 'RE' that best describes their business. We then make something from recycled materials that includes this word for their shop e.g. banner, badge, poster. For example, Oxfam has chosen 'REwear', Bet Fred, 'REsolute', Last Chance Hotel charity shop, 'REscue', Cornish Health Store, 'REfill' and Ladybird card shop 'RElations'. If you visit these shops look out for these pieces of 'artwear'. We are continuing to make great friendships with other traders in the town.

A day does not go by without someone dropping into our shop to tell us about the glory days of Redruth, particularly the clothes shops. We are encouraging people to think about what they want from their town centre in the future. At the end of the project we will produce a street map with these 'RE' messages.

We're also identifying women from Redruth who were involved in repairing clothes from the 1800s onwards. So far, our imagination has been captured by the lives of Louisa Andrew, umbrella mender, the Vivian sisters, milliners, Madame Gribble, draper, and Mary Glasson, dressmaker. These stories are often forgotten about despite the fact we all wear clothes from the moment we are born to the day we die. Cloth and fabric have changed history (think of the wool, linen, cotton, silk and synthetic industries and worldwide trading links). Indeed, storytelling is underpinned by metaphors from the clothing trades. We talk about spinning a yarn, fabricating a story, weaving a tale and following the thread.

We're planning a performance piece for International Repair Day on 18 October 2023. This will include a poet or story teller who can tie together traders' stories from the past, present and future.

We would like to bring together text and textiles in a community heritage and art project that bears witness to the clothes we wear, repair and care for.

Our celebration event will include all the local traders who have taken part in the project.

MAKE A MENDS
· OUR MANIFESTO ·
We Care, Repair & Share

SUSTAINABILITY RATHER THAN A THROWING AWAY CULTURE.
We will support people in caring, mending, repairing, altering and decorating their clothes. If it's broken we can fix it.

MULTI-CYCLING.
We're into any type of cycling, whether it's recycling, upcycling, downcycling, any sort of cycling - we like it!

VALUING RATHER THAN BUYING NEW.
Promoting the buying of second-hand clothes, wearing vintage, renting, swapping, swishing and making donations.

CREATIVITY.
Playing with textiles, crafting and being artful is something we all can have a go at. You don't need to have any previous experience. It's about sharing skills and ideas and having a bit of fun.

CITIZEN BEFORE CONSUMER.
Raising awareness of the problems of the clothing industry and its negative impact on our environment.

CRAFTIVISM - THE ART OF GENTLE PROTEST.
We use craftivism (craft + activism) to empower people of all ages and abilities. No one or act is too small to make a difference.

COMMUNITY ORIENTATED.
A sense of belonging is important to all of us. We aim to establish communities of creative, respectful and maybe a little rebellious menders!

Open Letter to Redruth

AGENTS 4 CHANGE

Dear Redruth,
You may know us as the Agents 4 Change, we built a skatepark, starred in a music video and dived into the history of our beloved town. But really, we're just worried and scared local youth screaming for change, fighting for change to come to this remote dumping ground.

Our journey so far:
The start, twelve youths, brought together for the same reason; our love for our home. We planned, argued, agreed, filmed and fought over our town, all with one thing in common, change.

Then Covid hit, but we pushed through it. Zoomed the rest of the way. We got the amazing news that at the end of all our hard work we were going to get our skatepark. That we had changed our town for the good.

Then the Agents broke apart. Originals were sucked into GCSEs, college and school life and by the time the call went back out, Agents 4 Change were nearly extinct.

We were called back to breathe life into rubbled Redruth, to plan a festival for our community, our home, but only one thing came to light. Between the poems and the creative exercises, between the discussion and the agreements we kept circling back to one phrase, one problem, one fear.

We don't feel safe in our own town, in our home!

We fought about it, gained new members all with the same message;
'Make our streets safe again.'

Redruth is our home but it's also a place of fear, of dark alleys and antisocial behaviour that makes young people second guess their safety. We looked at our town, with nowhere safe, no quiet place to go that we feel comfortable.

We talked about our own experiences, and how youths our age have been chased by people older than us and forced into shops like Wilko where we feel safe. How generational problems in our town have gotten parks nicknames like 'rough park' where even parents fear to send their children.

The Agents learnt that we had to reclaim our childhood, because life in Redruth took that from us, unable to be safe on streets where we feel threatened and fearful.

Redruth has such a vast history, some can be seen in the alleys, but even with the colours and art being plastered over them we still don't feel safe. Alleys are places many people our age fear, and we shouldn't, because they're quick and easy shortcuts to get us around our home, but because we don't feel safe we don't use them, we fear to use them.

**Dear Redruth,
we are youth, your youth, part of your community, your future and your history.**

Dear councillors and Cornwall Council, we are your citizens, your kids and workers, your school goers and soon to be working people and we don't feel safe.
We need your help. Will you leave us stranded, or will you help us fight?

Dear Mayor of Redruth, can you help us feel safe? Can you help us not live in fear?
Can you help us reclaim our town, reclaim our childhood, reclaim our lives?

Dear Redruth and the community, we love our home, we love our community, but our love doesn't stretch far when we fear walking down your streets, passing you by and walking with you. Change needs to happen, because the youth of Redruth are begging, and if we don't get the change we want, the change we need, we will fight for it. We will fight for our town, for our safety. And Redruth, you better know that we are coming for you, coming for change. And we will get it.

To making our streets safe again.
To making Redruth a better place.
To Agents 4 Change, fighting for the change this toppling town needs.

Thank You.

Redruth
I am the shoppers weaving in and out of stores
The multitude of charity shops
I hear the loud chatter
The occasional local musician
I feel the sense of community
The people who are proud to be Cornish
I smell the pasties from many different shops
I can feel the wellie dog statue tall and proud

Mo
aged 13

I hate you when people get drunk in the street
I hate you when I'm told I shouldn't go out late
in case of dangerous people.
I hate you when I get yelled at in the streets
I hate you when I feel like I can't go out
I hate you when I get bullied
I hate Redruth when I can't be myself.

Alice
aged 13

MESKLA
Brewyon Drudh

Mussel Gathering | Precious Fragment
Sovay Berriman

MESKLA | Brewyon Drudh is a multi-platform art work that uses sculpture and conversation to explore contemporary Cornish cultural identity & its relationship with heritage, land, and extraction industries, including tourism.

Conversation is vital to MESKLA, and has taken place through workshops, podcasts, a symposium, public talks, and an exhibition, considering issues of authenticity, fractured culture, the links between identity, land and labour, indigeneity, language and intangible culture.

Through the MESKLA project I engage with people to seek and record their views on Cornish cultural identity, and how the discussion relates to broader contexts - historically, nationally and globally.

Sculpture is central to my art practice, and an important part of MESKLA. Sculpture takes up space, and within MESKLA it becomes a physical place holder for Cornish identity and culture. The workshop conversations encourage open dialogue and listening, creating space for participants to be able to articulate their views, and consider different perspectives and experiences. Through talking whilst making, participants are given an opportunity to access different modes of thinking, the variety and nature of the found and reclaimed materials used inspires and challenges in new and sometimes alternative ways. It is essential that participants are able to play freely without judgement, and the pace of the conversations is unhurried, to allow time to unpick areas that anyone might find uncomfortable. All making is powerful, having permission and opportunity to be creative with no direct instruction reinforces that all voices, views and experiences are important.

The future of MESKLA will continue this deep exploration of individual relationships to Cornish identity, while also questioning more structural factors. I'm planning conversations that will look at the impact and meaning of the Cornish diaspora, and power structures such as monarchy and land ownership, as well as the significance of links between the Celtic nations. MESKLA will continue to question how we maintain being a modern, open, embracing culture, making space for those who feel the import of ancestry, and those who choose Cornwall as their home and identifying culture.

The most powerful findings from the conversations and stories of MESKLA | Brewyon Drudh rubbish sculpture making and conversation workshops has been a sense of belonging. This has been naturally varied for each person taking part, but many seem to focus upon three areas - community, ancestry and land.

COMMUNITY

Participants have spoken about their experience and feeling of strength of community and how that gives them a sense of belonging.

People have mentioned a few different physical centres of community in Redruth - places such as St Rumon's Social Club, CN4C - The Elms, the Butter Market, Krowji, Auction House, Ringrose's and Lucky's, for instance. A lot of people have also spoken about the Methodist Church and how the Methodist community is welcoming and embracing, even for people who don't necessarily relate to the religious aspect of Methodism, they still strongly identify with the community.

The power of these centres in bringing divergent and intersecting groups together really helps define a feeling of Redruth community.

Through running the workshops in a range of venues within the town I found that different but parallel groupings experienced similar senses of community within Redruth as a whole. Some people expressed that they felt strongly connected to the town by just being a part of it, but not particularly having any 'leading' role. I'm particularly interested in this, and how the simplest of our everyday or mundane activities can be markers of identity or belonging.

Within St Rumon's Social Club I chatted with a participant who identifies as Irish, although they grew up in Cornwall and had a Cornish father and family. They told me about how their mother was Irish and that is who they gained their identity from. Their mother had passed on her culture, whereas their Cornish relatives didn't really imbue a spirit of Cornish culture, and they didn't behave as inclusive and accepting. This illustrated the strength of the role of community in developing a feeling and understanding of cultural identity.

Redruth is a place where people can pull together, where people are close, where there is a strong concentration of Cornish identifying people, and yet also a healthy movement of people from many other places into the town, who are also committed to the community as a whole and to the town; a place they call home.

ANCESTRY

For some it was very important to be able to be around other Cornish people, and to have grown up in and around 'more traditional Cornish culture'. They have said there's an aspect of communication that is different, that they know and understand, that isn't solely communicated with words or language particularly. It is a form of communication that is familiar, that makes them feel at home, and that they know, almost bodily.

Many participants who have moved to Cornwall as adults spoke of feeling a strong sense of belonging here that they hadn't felt in the places they'd grown-up; of how they want to become Cornish in time; of how they respect Cornish culture and are proud of it. A participant who came along to a market drop-in workshop told me all about their spouse and children being Cornish and that they were proud of that for them, but that they themselves didn't feel they were Cornish. Their identity was rooted elsewhere.

I have had people tell me that they don't feel allowed to be Cornish, whether they moved here as adults or children, because they were born elsewhere. These contributors talk of their choice of Cornishness as part of their identity, but of how they feel inhibited in claiming that.

I have been glad to receive positive feedback in relation to how the podcast conversations have explored the difficult balance between the sense of immediate community and deep rooted ancestry - "I may not be Cornish but after listening I felt comfortable in my connection to contemporary cultural threads in the fabric of Cornish life." and "It was an excellent podcast - with many salient points, and it's got to be a winner for emmets like myself who love Cornish culture but can feel like a bit of an outsider-tourist even after 20 years. It made me feel I might genuinely engage with Cornish culture despite a fear of a kind of tacky appropriation."

The sustaining power of industrial heritage persists. During a workshop at St Rumon's Social Club I heard personal histories of working in the mining industry, and particularly at Crofty. A young person spoke of their regret at not having that traditional trade to go into anymore. They felt a sadness at not being able to follow in the tradition of their family in working in the mining industry. This sense of ancestral loss seemed to run deep in Redruth, the industries that helped shape a global perception of Cornwall for millennia still shaping the feeling of belonging and identity. However, there were many other participants who were keen to move-on from these perceptions, to carve a different future.

LAND

Many people have spoken about a connection to the land of Cornwall as the thing that gives them identity, belonging, and makes them feel at home; a connection to place and personal histories. One of the first people who took part in the project, who had moved here as an adult, told me that they claimed Cornishness as this was where they belonged, the land was their home.

A visitor to a Redruth Market drop-in workshop began to cry as they told me of the connection they felt to the land where they had grown up, that they knew that they walked paths that their ancestors had, and that connection gave them strength and made them feel loved. Others have spoken of how they feel they are part of the land in Cornwall, that it is part of them, that they are 'built' for it in some way.

Another participant spoke of how they would at times feel connected to the land of Cornwall, but that that sense of belonging would be undermined by racist comments and questioning their right to connection to place. This participant did speak of the sea connecting the places of their heritage, and places where they have worked around the globe. They spoke of a strong feeling of home with the proximity of the sea, that it is a body of welcoming.

Then there are those who spoke of not having Cornish ancestry, but who moved to Cornwall as children, during formative years. These participants detailed experience of the influence of the land upon the development of their identities, and again that it gave them a strong sense of home, of the familiar, of belonging.

Many participants who've moved to Cornwall as adults spoke of how a connection with the land in Cornwall was what drew and held them here. A participant described how the land had never told them to go 'home', and that when they were out walking they felt a sense of belonging.

The intensity of feeling about identity and connection to place was palpable in these conversations.

For me the project grew from a strong sense of grief, that I felt like something that was fundamental to who I am was disappearing, and more than just simply disappearing, it was being actively ignored and treated as though it didn't matter, at times as though it were a joke, whilst simultaneously being repackaged and commodified. I found this difficult for a number of political and personal reasons.

Whilst growing up my family was viewed as 'different', we didn't fit societal norms, and communities we lived within actively did not accept us. Knowing I was Cornish in an ancestral, ancient way connected me to something that gave me power to overcome the restrictions or limitations of my local community. The connection to the Celtic nations network gave me a strong and positive international outlook.

My Cornish identity has always been powerful to me. From a teen I connected to my Cornish identity as something pagan, elemental, anti-establishment and anti-colonial. I didn't need acceptance or inclusion from people, in any community, for that identity, that I had it from the land of my ancestors, gave me so much strength and independence. I recognise the huge privilege and gift I have through that experience and I hold on to it as it helped me survive the mainly misogynist, heteronormative, homophobic, classist, and abelist society I grew up in.

My Cornish identity has shaped my work and personal life, from campaigning work in the early 1990s, which included Pennskol Kernow - a campaign for a university for Cornwall, and awareness raising of housing needs for young people and those identifying as no fixed abode; through to my practice as an artist and how I research, make work and organise events and projects.

In recent years observing that Cornish culture has been increasingly undermined and parodied has been frustrating and stressing in equal measure. The transition of Cornwall from industrial centre to tourist playground having gathered pace to the point of feeling like there was little room left for those who identify as Cornish, or who don't have access to 'lifestyle' Cornwall.

This reminds me of experiences of my youth, with a difference now being that I am at a moment where I do have access to a form of power and privilege, and I understand it is my responsibility to use that privilege to ask questions and challenge the mediated status quo. The significance of the stories and experiences shared by MESKLA | Brewyon Drudh participants over 2022 has reinforced and validated my approach this work.

The next phase of the MESKLA project will continue taking up and making space with rubbish sculptures and open conversations that articulate, recognise, and celebrate contemporary Cornish cultural identity in all the multitude of ways it exists.

Redruth Press

Redruth Press is a collaboration between two local artists, Caroline Wilkins & Tony Minnion, who both live and work in Redruth.

a vibrant democratic voice for people.

Redruth Press uses screen printing and the traditional function of a poster as protest and call for action on community issues and utilises the historic place that print has for providing a vibrant democratic voice for people.

They use a mobile screen printing workshop to instigate conversations at different places and events in Cornwall that engage with as many people as possible. They also run workshop sessions with hands-on engagement sharing accessible poster printing processes.

As part of the Redruth Unlimited project they delivered public facing events, asking local people for their opinions on a range of topics. The artists asked questions that stimulated progressive and positive responses about the town, its heritage and its future, steering away from what was wrong with it and emphasising what was great about it, what makes us proud of it and what we can all do now to make it even better.

Tony and Caroline used the responses they gathered to produce instant posters so that people can see their ideas come to life. They have also run workshops across the community targeting the offer to groups that may feel disempowered and marginalised. The posters produced from both ways of working were then fly posted on two poster walls in the centre of Redruth, changing and developing over the year of the project. These displays have brightened two run-down building fronts in the centre of town and have spread a positive message of change and hope.

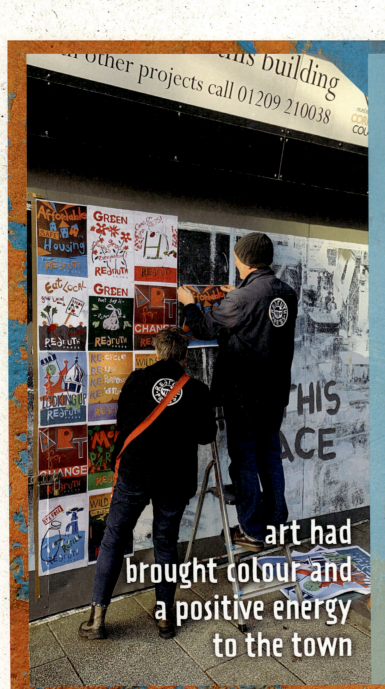

art had brought colour and a positive energy to the town

At one event, back in the spring, Caroline spoke with a woman who was visiting from Australia. She happened to be in Redruth as she moved from train to bus on her way to walk part of the coastal path. She recounted how she had made the same transition five years before and how Redruth had stuck in her mind for all the wrong reasons. She had found the town to be grey and drab and her family had adopted 'Redruth' as a term for somewhere you would not want to stay for long.

She was eager to tell them how wrong they had been and of her delight in finding a town so transformed. The market day was full of community, of friendliness and of creativity. She could see that art had brought colour and a positive energy to the town.

As a legacy for this creative consultation across the community, Redruth Press have produced a large-scale hoarding featuring a 6 x 4 metre enlargement of one of their posters which now acts as a visual gateway to the town, spreading the positive message that Redruth is 'Looking Up'. They have also transformed the poster walls into permanent printed displays featuring every poster that has been produced over the 18 month project.

15 Draughts Later

Ollie Mcfarlane and James Darcy

15 Draughts Later is a storytelling project aimed at creating local legends and myths by drawing on the local history, then performing them in pubs. We started in Redruth finding stories about all sorts: government curfews, breweries, arson, whatever we could find. Then we built the stories into fantastical legends. Pigs who go on a drunken rampage and all end up in prison, an enraged Cornish nationalist burning down 'unwanted centres of commerce', a poor local maid who simply cannot catch a break. We then took the stories and performed them in the local pubs and bars in Redruth. We hope that we will help preserve and breathe new life into Redruth's fabulous history.

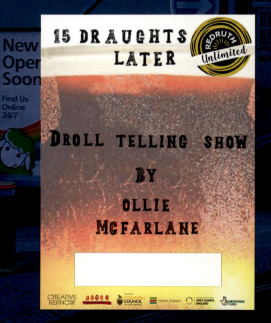

Operation Goodnight

Ollie Mcfarlane

All was not well on the Close Hill estate in Redruth, or so it seemed to PC Griffin. Operation Goodnight had descended and the good people of Redruth were all of a flutter. 16 and unders were required to be back at home by 9pm. 9PM! The teenagers of the great town had plenty to say. "I think it sucks cos it ain't even gonna work, they're telling us that we've got to be back in bed by nine o' clock every night, this shouldn't even be legal!" cried one teenage resident. "I'll be laughing at the police, doing anything that tickles my fancy," snorted another. A third teenager did a wheelie on his bike, defiance and anarchy were in the air.

PC Griffin had dreamed up Operation Goodnight in response to kids on Close Hill, as young as eight, loitering on the streets late into the night. And on July 25th 2008 it was all about to kick off.

Nine o'clock came, and PC Griffin drove slowly around the estate, fearing his good idea would be resigned to being a bad case study in police school.

But to his surprise, not a teenager was in sight. And in a week, crime was down 98%. Perhaps all was well in the Close Hill estate after all.

TREASURES OF REDRUTH

A TALE OF REDRUTH
Phil Kincaid

The 'Treasures of Redruth' event that took place on 25th June 2022 has a story to tell. For quite some time I realised that the Market Hall of Redruth was inadvertently blocking trade, disconnecting the town centre from The Buttermarket due to its underuse. The empty view from both sides of what had become a relatively abandoned space was stopping people passing through. My proposal to the council was to encourage traffic via a series of handmade textile banners that celebrate the past, present and future heritage of our town, rich in history and populated by fascinating characters.

Casual research quickly led to Fanny Moody. I had heard her name before, knowing she was an operatic soprano of some considerable fame. Unearthing photographs of her proved effortless. Dressed in typical Edwardian theatrical costume, she seemed generous and warm, smiling out from the past. I needed to know more – to get to know her.

Born in Redruth, Fanny established a touring opera company with her husband that built a considerable reputation in both Britain and Europe. However, she would often return to her place of birth to raise money for local charities through her singing. In her time she was a treasured celebrity. It's sad to think that there are no known recordings of her and we can only imagine how she charmed her audiences. Whilst sketching some ideas for this first banner, I fantasised about the idea of bringing Fanny back to life: the image of the ghost of Fanny persisted. Being theatrical, I was determined to make this happen. This is where our modern day story truly begins.

Further research and discussion settled on three further banners for the Market Hall space. First of all it seemed obvious to me that I should organise a collaborative piece involving local artists and craftspeople with the open title of 'Treasures of Redruth'. The resulting work incorporated images of local architecture, landscapes and emotionally responsive abstracts. Kitchie George was mentioned – a well-known and respected street dweller from years gone by - as well as the long lost phrase 'Hockings for Stockings: Knights for Tights'.

On the back of the banner I listed local businesses and famous people born in Redruth including Kristin Scott Thomas, Mick Fleetwood and Aphex Twin amongst others. Because ceramics feature heavily in the history of the town, such as a large pottery where Jim's Cash and Carry now resides, I designed a banner made from small pieces of clay with contributions from local, non-arty people. Last of all, I had stumbled upon a character known as 'Charlie Bruno: Eccentric Comedian' from around the same time as Fanny. The luxury of knowing so much about her was in direct contrast to Charlie.

Necessary meetings with the town council were all part of the fun. Not everyone had heard of Fanny but they were fascinated by the idea of celebrating her and returning her to Redruth. During the process of designing the banner the Fanny jokes persisted, particularly when people got wind of the project. 'Fancy a look at my Fanny?' was a common phrase. There was, at least, always a smile.

I literally had one haunting photograph and nothing else. No amount of digging for more information yielded results. Yet, the photograph said so much. Not knowing anything about him — other than the fact he must have been important enough to have his photo taken — was precisely what made him captivating.

The weeks rolled by and my sewing fingers were getting sore from the heavy duty work of piecing together the various textiles and it was time to think how we would frame the banners in an event celebrating our wonderful town.

My mother was an extraordinary craftswoman and artist who taught me everything I know. Over the years she produced a large amount of works, fine in their detail and various. For her it was the process that mattered and so habitually stored everything in drawers or in boxes. My habit in turn was to show my friends what she could do. This got me thinking; surely there must be many treasures hidden away behind closed doors in Redruth — as in every town — that deserve to be seen and admired by others. So the shoutout was shouted out and the revealed objects with their accompanying stories were given new life.

Soon there were enough items to warrant a museum-esque display — for one rare day only — to illustrate the tender passions of the citizens of our town in the safety of the covered Market Hall.

A collection of vintage and slightly faded programmes from the many stage shows produced by Redruth Amateur Operatic Society encouraged conversations about cherished individuals lost as well as the exhilaration of performance either as children or as enthusiastic adults. Fanny would have heartily approved.

The delight of revealing a sequinned ballgown from the 1950s ('She had many husbands but kept the dress') was matched by a small, smooth almond that had been carried through the first World War by a cherished grandfather. Other treasures included photographs and objets trouvés, amongst them small items that had either been gifted by or to my mother including a dandelion clock captured in resin and the Bakelite box my grandmother carried her hairgrips in and now contains the baby teeth of my first dog. A tiny lizard skeleton was described simply as 'Found it: liked it' which chimed nicely with Charlie.

The day of the event was busy. It was obviously a responsibility taking care of so many Redruth Treasures that were arranged in a way that made them look as if they had been 'unwrapped' — only to be all too soon hidden away again at the end of the day. Our audience found the atmosphere of the exhibition captivating and, indeed, stories were exchanged as was hoped.

But what of Fanny?

At a given time I spoke of Fanny and her success, contemplating the idea of being able, somehow, to hear her famed dulcets. It was then that the ghost of Fanny appeared, hushed at first from the distance of The Buttermarket. Gasps were audible. As she sang she could see the tears in people's eyes which prompted tears of her own. It was after she had completed her programme of beautiful arias and her banner unveiled that one of the exhibition artists quietly told me that one of them sung so close and so tenderly had helped considerably in the journey of his grief for his mother. If only for this reason the whole event was a considerable success and an audience member is quoted as saying 'The best event that Redruth has seen'.

Stret an Levow Street of Voices

In 2021 Annamaria Murphy, Sue Hill and Ciaran Clarke were commissioned by Sound UK to create an immersive sound walk for Redruth. In the challenging environment framed by the pandemic, they tracked the stories embedded in the town and its folk, recorded voices, bells, animals, birds, weather and crafted a sound journey that zig-zagged between contemporary lived experience, the deep past and living memory.

Historic England worked with the National Trust and Sound UK to bring hidden histories and stories to life across six High Street Heritage Action Zones. The Redruth High Street Sound Walk is part of a series of self-guided, immersive sound walks to take listeners on a journey of discovery. Listeners are supported by an illustrated map while they take a self-guided route at their own pace.

Writers:	Annamaria Murphy & Sue Hill
Sound:	Ciaran Clarke
Research:	Tamsin Spargo, Will Tremayne, Hetty Bevington
Song and additional lyrics:	Claire Ingleheart
Sound UK:	Maija Handover, Polly Eldridge
Carn to Cove Project Co-ordination:	Claire Marshall
Photography:	Josh Morse (www.cornishphoto.co.uk)

historicengland.org.uk/get-involved/high-street-culture/sound-walks/redruth

PRODIGAL SON

Sue Hill

The great stores in Redruth – West End, Cockings, John Knights - were all owned by members of a faith brotherhood. The Christian Brethren worshipped together, but traded in competition with each other. Good men, they ran tight ships and believed that humanity could be improved with the values of Family, Work, Clean Living and Great Shopping.

Imagine a boy, child of the Brethren, growing up in the 60s and 70s. No discos and drink for him, no dancing, no rock, no flirting, no sly cigarettes with the shop girls on the roof terrace of the store. No, it's the Meeting House for prayer three times on Sundays, and every day for four days over Easter, when the other lads from school would be out on the randan, enjoying the first warmth of spring. No girlfriends for him, some of the Brethren have arranged marriages...

And when he's not at school or prayer he's in the shop, learning the family trade. He blushes easily, this boy. Mrs T, farmer's wife, coming down the sweeping store staircase towards him, raises her skirt to her chin - 'Ere, Mr Knight, got any like these ave ee?' and at the sight of what he calls her 'harvest festivals, you know, all safely gathered in', he blushes furiously.

His future path seems set. But then something breaks in him. There is a storm, a biblical flood that sweeps through the centre of Redruth wrecking and contaminating everything in its path. The store and its stock are ruined. He cannot face the endless task of repairing and repainting and somehow, aged 17, manages to get sent to London for 'training'.

He is away for three years. It's another life he says. When he returns he sets up one of the first boutiques in Cornwall on the top floor of the store, painted vibrant orange and purple, swagged with thick nautical rope, stocked with the most ravishing clothes. They make women feel and look glorious, splendid, beautiful, sexy, modern. It's a kind of rebellion.

Ever the innovator, in a land used to tucking sheets and blankets in tightly, like swaddling, he introduces the duvet. He has to demonstrate their use to the Townswomen's Guild, changing the duvet cover, fluffing and plumping. Even after his experiences in the city, this is an encounter fraught with embarrassment. The mature ladies of the town relish his discomfort, teasing and giggling with merciless double entendres. He still blushes at the memory. You can take the boy out of the Brethren, but maybe you can't take the Brethren out of the boy.

EMILY KNUCKEY AND THE CARPET

Annamaria Murphy

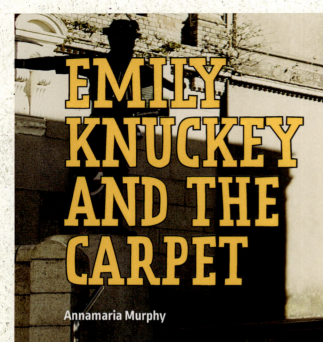

Back Lane West. Imagine the aromas.
Contraband alcohol. Mahogany, a drink of Gin and Black Treacle.
Kiddlywink Broth: whole onion stewed with a bit of bacon and kidney,
Eggy hot: a delicious concoction of an egg in warm beer.
Kiddlywinks: illegal drinking dens, sweat, smoke and gutters, chamberpots and ale.
Illegal lace, tea and silk purchased in Back Lane West.
Customers from Mrs Rodda's brothel,
herself a Left Behind Woman.

A heady mix.

And sounds.
Emily Knuckey, famous for foul language and disorderly behaviour.
She spoke the language of the street, sang sonnets of poverty, argued in arias of swearing.
Emily Knuckey. By the time she was twenty one, she had been arrested twenty three times, so violent when roused, that policemen bore the scratches of her anger on their faces and the bruises of her rage on their shins.
On one occasion, her fury was so hot that she could not be taken. Her arms flailed like a tree in a storm, her legs kicked like a bitten donkey.

The arresting officers could not still her. So they wrapped her in a carpet and fastened it with several belts.
She was taken kicking and screaming to the station at Redruth, loaded onto the train and delivered to the court in Bodmin still in her carpet straight jacket.
We don't know of her judgement, but to Emily, this may have been the only time she'd come near to a carpet.
Maybe, once she was in her cell, she laid the carpet out, and walked upon it?

I hope so.

CONTRIBUTOR BIOGRAPHIES

SOVAY BERRIMAN's work is rooted in their experience of being Cornish, their culture's shifting identity, and the mutability yet power of a sense of place. Evolution, domestic and industrial use of the natural environment, alongside performance platforms and dance floors, inform the abstract and semi-fantastical sculptural structures and events they build.
In their practice Sovay is committed to questioning balances of power; they use visual art as a structure and prompt for action and discussion, focusing on areas they want to learn more about. They invite contributors and participants into their work at opportune moments when collaborating.
In 2015 they trained as a plumbing and heating engineer and work in the construction industry alongside their art activity. Their experiences in this line of work have allowed them to develop the critical socio-economic and political aspects of their practice, particularly in relation to environment, care and the labour of making. They have a studio at Krowji.
sovayberriman.co.uk

SARA CLASPER was born in Sunderland in 1964, she now lives on the north coast of Cornwall. She has lived in various places prior to settling in Cornwall, Oxford, Lake District, London and Newcastle. She is a keen climate activist and has joined two other women opening h.q. Make A Mends in Redruth Spring 2022.
She studied BA Art/Art History in Oxford, qualified as an art teacher and has exhibited her work at home and abroad. She now stitches her way along life sending messages through clothes.

AMANDA HARRIS is Director of Kernow Education Arts Partnership and founder of The Writers' Block with Annamaria Murphy and Helen Reynolds. She grew up near Helston and has worked in the arts in Cornwall for over 35 years. She is passionate about the power of the arts to change lives. In particular the power of the imagination through creating and sharing of story. She has written a novel *Behind the Lines* and collaborated with photographer Steve Tanner on *A Space to Write* exploring the spaces where writers choose to work.
thewritersblock.org.uk

SUE HILL was born and educated in Cornwall and has worked with numerous companies from Kneehigh to the Eden Project. She has a particular interest in the role of art and culture in building and sustaining communities. She has created the Mudmaid and the Giant at Heligan with her brother, re-imagined Tom Bawcock's Eve with Annamaria Murphy, performed in Kneehigh shows at Trelissick, Trelowarren, The Minack, Sterts, Hall for Cornwall & The National Theatre. She is a founder member of WildWorks making site specific theatre in Cornwall and beyond. She was Artistic Director at the Eden Project, commissioning Cornish artists and she designed the head of the Man Engine.

PHIL KINCAID was born near London into an artistic family and benefitted from a liberal 70s education steeped in the visual and performing arts. As part of the Thalidomide generation, celebrating 'difference' was natural and held him in good stead in the years to come during a long career as a therapist and award winning support worker. Phil studied music at the *Royal Academy of Music* in London and Theatre and Performance/Drama in Education with *Plymouth University*. He is also a trained Celebrant.
As well as the Arts featuring prominently in his career, teaching has also been important. His mission through teaching is to enable people to unearth and develop their self-confidence whilst also mentoring on the principles of 'Person Centred' support and true inclusion. This is best illustrated by *Mining Exchange Studios CIC* which he created and currently runs. Redruth now boasts an important beating 'heart' that rejects discrimination and judgement and celebrates difference in all its glory.

OLLIE MCFARLANE is an actor, director and aerialist based in Cornwall. He is a member of The Story Republic and has worked with companies such as Kneehigh, Wildworks and the Barbican. Ollie's other interests include history, theology, and weightlifting.

TONY MINNION is a contemporary landscape painter who paints on the Cornish North Coast. He learned to screen print at 16 and has used it for political and social engagement across the community ever since. He works in combination with digital processes to create individual and large collaborative artworks for public display in various forms including banners, flags and hoardings. He also specialises in working with people who are neurologically diverse.
redruthpress.co.uk

ANNAMARIA MURPHY is the Artistic Director & Lead Writer of The Writers' Block and The Story Republic. She was a long term member of Kneehigh Theatre most recently as a writer and producer of their final series of events 'Random Acts of Art'. Amongst others, she has worked with C-scape Dance, Theatre Alibi, Little Angel Theatre, Rogue, and Stuff and Nonsense. Her writing for BBC Radio 4's 'Curious Under the Stars' was highly acclaimed. Anna writes from her shed in the garden, where she hoards interesting objects with which to inspire her characters.

DR SARAH PERRY BA (Hons), PhD, DClinPsy is Cornish and grew up on a farm situated in the Tamar valley. She studied Psychology and earned both a PhD and then Doctorate in Clinical Psychology. She started out professionally as a Health and Social Care researcher working at a number of universities. Then she trained to be a Clinical Psychologist, enabling her to join the NHS and work in both children and adult mental health services. She then became self-employed as a consultant psychologist, working for a number of organisations helping them with service evaluation projects. She gradually developed her crafting skills and started to sell what she made: This eventually led to craftivism, starting a Community Interest Company and opening Make A Mends in Redruth.

RIFT

are Felix Mortimer and Joshua Nawras. Felix and Josh have worked together for 14 years producing plays, festivals, events and running arts spaces in Hoxton, Poplar, Tottenham and Shoreditch. RIFT relocated to Cornwall to work on turning Redruth's Old Library into an arts and culture hub, now called The Ladder, which they hope will become a hub for the performing arts for Cornwall.

TRIFLE GATHERING PRODUCTIONS

produce comedy theatre, immersive theatrical experiences and bespoke community arts projects with a focus on social change. They are a core creative team of three women: Sally Crooks, Kyla Goodey and Hannah Stephens, who have a dual practice in theatre and therapeutic arts. Trifle Gathering's brand of anarchic satire brings the community closer through a shared appreciation of the absurdity of life. They tell peculiar tales exploring the secret worlds of life's unsung heroes!

CAROLINE WILKINS

is a contemporary artist who works with a variety of print processes on and with objects to make large scale installations. With over 25 years of art teaching experience including many spent working with children excluded from mainstream education she now delivers printmaking classes for adults, works on commissioned art projects and exhibits her contemporary art practice.
cwprintmaker.co.uk

AGENTS 4 CHANGE,

We Love Redruth, is a vital youth project designed to encourage youth activism, empowering the young people of Redruth to have their say in the future of their town.

REFERENCES

THE HAUNTING

I will endlessly walk through this building. Through door after door, room after room and creeping along corridors. I run up and down the stairs, my hand lightly trailing the polished bend of the banister. The one you slid and shrieked down as a child, then raced back up again, your footsteps tracing the curve of the wood like fingers along a sleeping woman's spine. You stood in awe in front of the enormous, gleaming wooden desks in the records room. At least, they seemed enormous to you. The work of giants and the reverence of the written word. Until, the spell was broken and the curiosity of childhood won. "We played pingpong on them instead," you said. The caretaker lived in the basement then. I don't think he ever once shooed you away as you bounded in and played each day.

Now you tend to the garden, whack back the weeds and work and work at the ground that surrounds this place. I must seem like a child to you, with my bags of curiosity leading me on to poke, prod and pull at the threads which tie it all together. To tease out and touch the sanctity of the site.

"It's haunted," someone said.
"It's not." he said.
"It is" they all said.
"We each heard it," they said.
"Heard what?" he said.
"Hello" they said, "It whispered to the two of us."
"Bollocks," he said.
"It's true!" they said, "There I was, sat on the loo and it whispered in my ear."
"Mine too." the other said.
"You were sitting on a loo as well and a ghost spoke to you?" he said.
"No." the other one said, "I was outside."
"Bollocks" he said and walked off.

In a way, you are the caretaker now. You showed me the room in the basement where you store your tools and the spot where you sometimes fall asleep – so exhausted from the efforts of the day and the enormity of the task. You love it really, I can tell.

I watch as in the garden you work away together. One building and shaping and the other pruning and planting. The child who grew up and the man who shapes and builds.

"Morning!" I say.
You smile back and say, "Hello."

Name: Olivia Lowry

Parents:

Activities: Writer-in-resid[ence]

THE WRITERS' BLOCK

Thanks to our funders

As well as

Cornwall Community Foundation
Redruth High Street Heritage Action Zone
Redruth Cultural Consortium

Historic England
HM Government
National Trust

People's Postcode Lottery
Postcode Earth Trust
National Lottery Heritage Fund

Thank you to

All the wonderful project leaders, artists, writers and everyone who has shared their story in so many ways. In addition:

Stephen Childs and Rachael Mia Allen at
The Redruth Drapery
Ben Read at Beats and Roots
Sam White at Redruth Town Council
Claire Tripp at Azook
Ross Williams at Redruth Revival
Rose Barnecut
Eric Morse
Jack, Max and Jasper Morrison
Phil Hosken

Neil Gay
Vanessa Moyle
Karren Mann
Coastline Housing
Shallal
Gwealan Tops
Kresen Kernow
Town Centre traders and cafes
Redruth Rugby Club

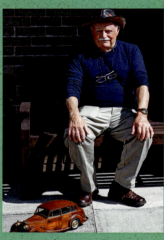

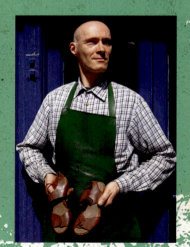